THE AUTHOR

Duane T. Gish is Associate Director of the Institute for Creation Research in San Diego. With a Ph.D. from the University of California (Berkeley) and many years of experience in scientific research, Dr. Gish is widely known as an outstanding lecturer and debater on the scientific evidence for special creation. He is author of the best-selling book, *Evolution? The Fossils Say NO!* and a booklet, *Have You Been Brainwashed?*, with worldwide distribution of over two million copies.

Happy Birthday Noah!
Love, Edy
Proverbs 3:5+6
5/14/88

No one living in the world today
has ever seen a dinosaur —
a live one, that is. A few folks even
doubt that anything like a dinosaur
really ever lived at all; but they did —
long, long ago.

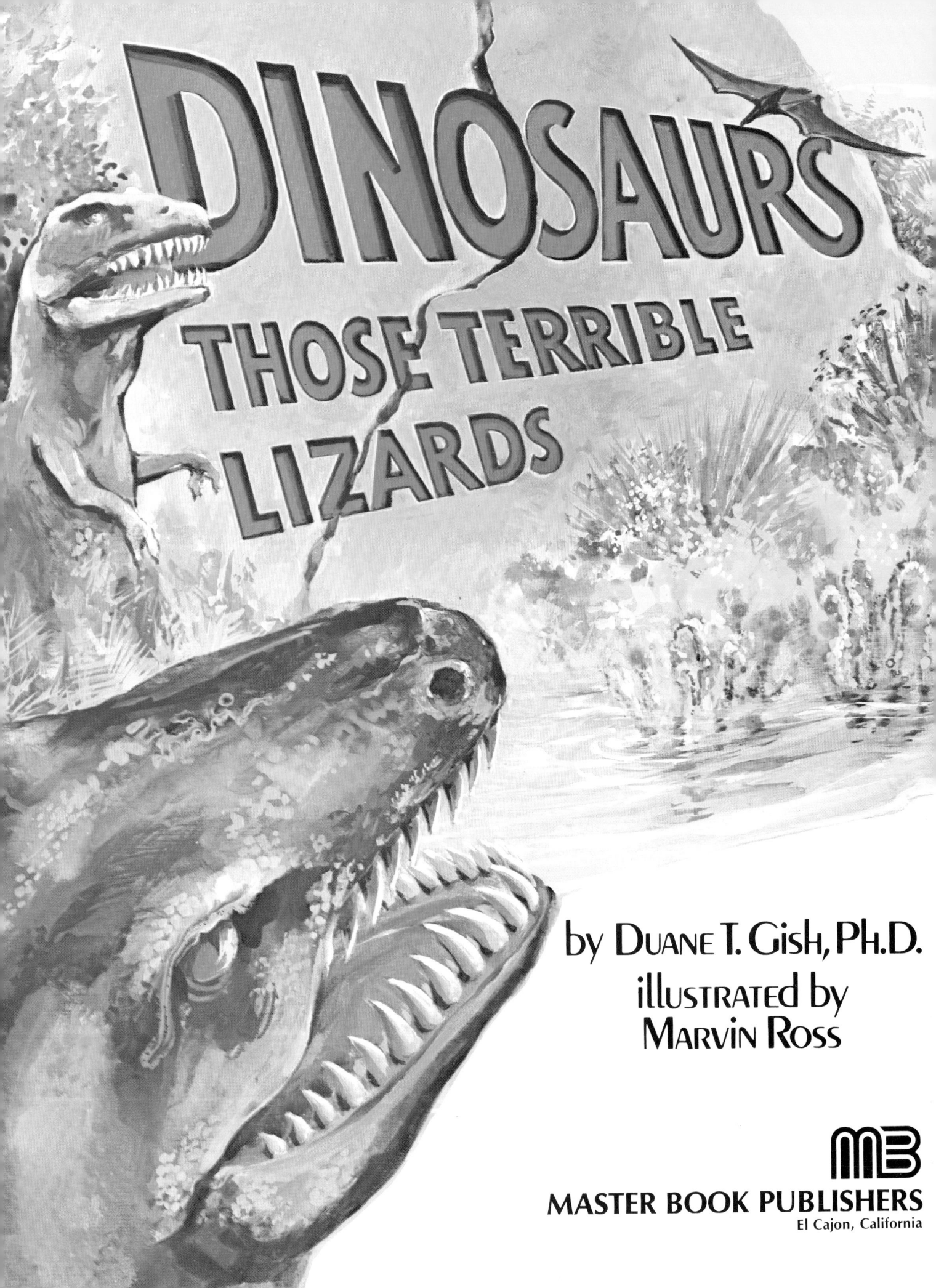

DINOSAURS
THOSE TERRIBLE LIZARDS

by Duane T. Gish, Ph.D.

illustrated by
Marvin Ross

MB

MASTER BOOK PUBLISHERS
El Cajon, California

DINOSAURS: Those Terrible Lizards

Copyright © 1977

MASTER BOOK PUBLISHERS

A Division of CLP, Inc.
P.O. Box 1606
El Cajon, California 92022

First printing, September 1977
Second printing, October 1978
Third printing, February 1980
Fourth printing, February 1982
Fifth printing, February 1984
Sixth printing, November 1985
Seventh printing, March 1986

Library of Congress Catalog
Card Number 77-89152
ISBN 0-89051-039-3

Cataloging in Publication Data
Gish, Duane Tolbert, 1921-
   Dinosaurs: those terrible lizards.
   1. Dinosauria—Juvenile literature.   2. Paleontology.
   I. Title. II. Ross, Marvin, ill.
         568.19   77-89152

Printed in Hong Kong

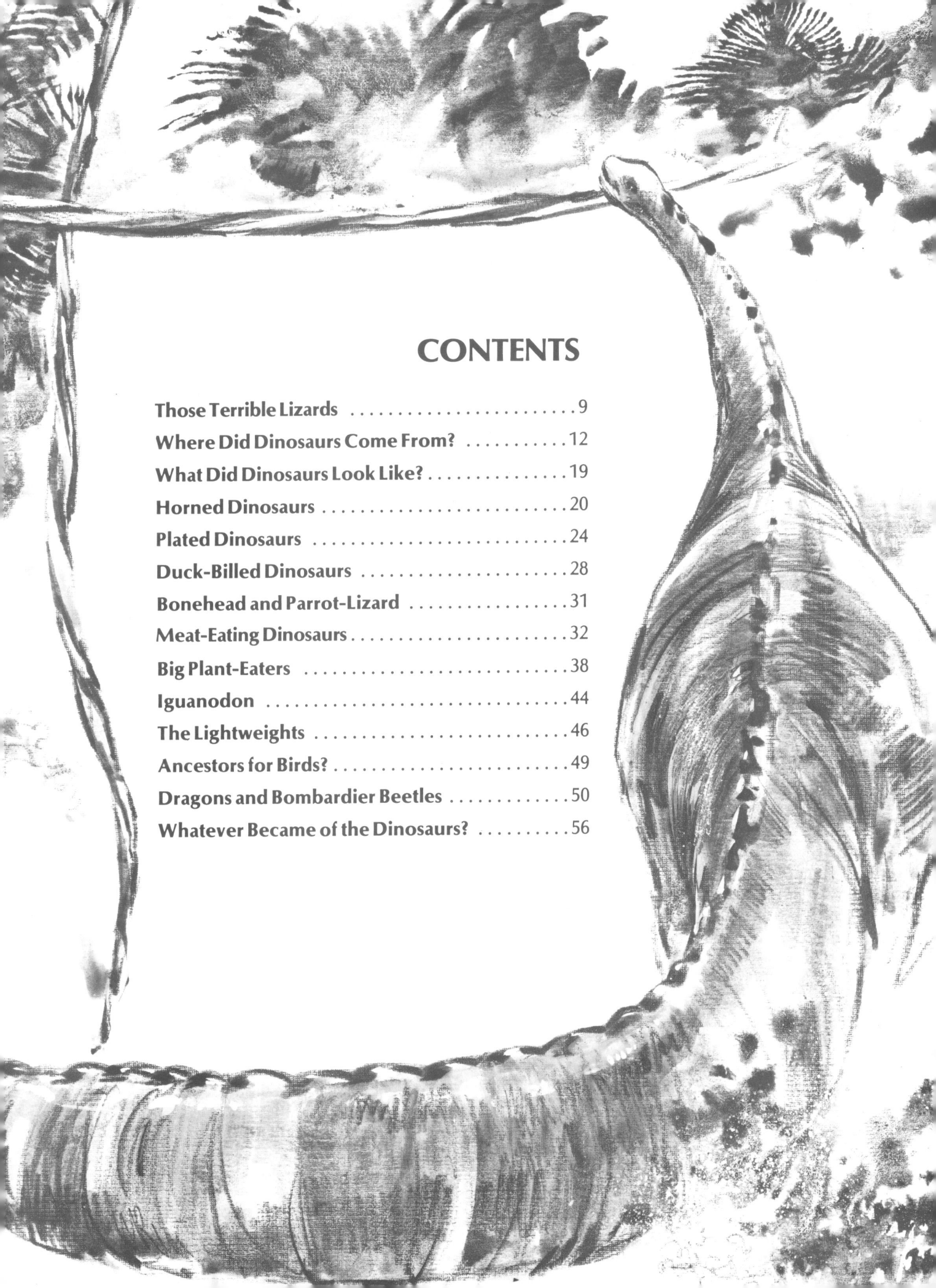

CONTENTS

Those Terrible Lizards 9

Where Did Dinosaurs Come From? 12

What Did Dinosaurs Look Like? 19

Horned Dinosaurs 20

Plated Dinosaurs 24

Duck-Billed Dinosaurs 28

Bonehead and Parrot-Lizard 31

Meat-Eating Dinosaurs 32

Big Plant-Eaters 38

Iguanodon 44

The Lightweights 46

Ancestors for Birds? 49

Dragons and Bombardier Beetles 50

Whatever Became of the Dinosaurs? 56

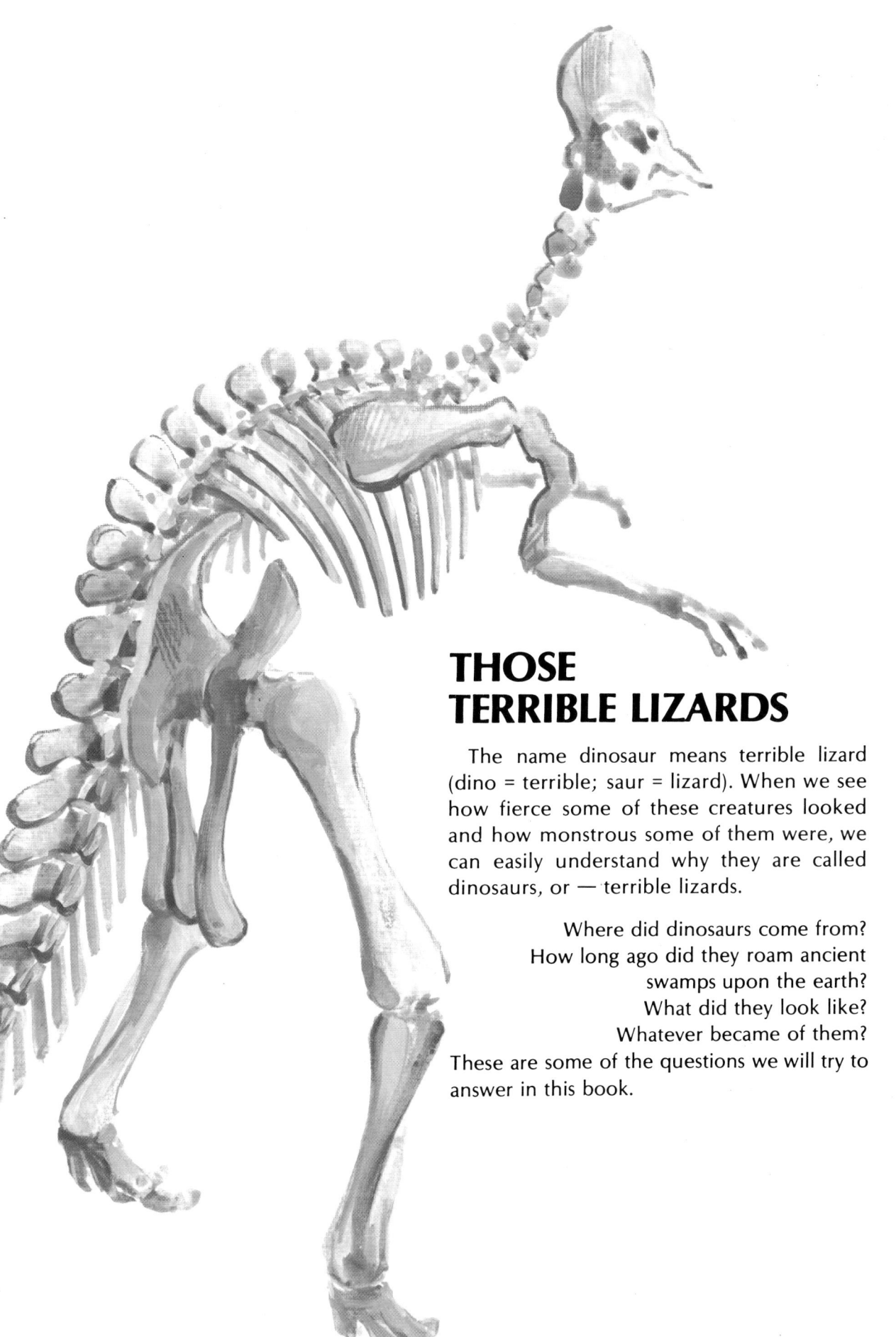

THOSE TERRIBLE LIZARDS

The name dinosaur means terrible lizard (dino = terrible; saur = lizard). When we see how fierce some of these creatures looked and how monstrous some of them were, we can easily understand why they are called dinosaurs, or — terrible lizards.

Where did dinosaurs come from?
How long ago did they roam ancient
swamps upon the earth?
What did they look like?
Whatever became of them?
These are some of the questions we will try to answer in this book.

Where do we find dinosaur fossils? In many parts of the world — from the Arctic island of Spitzbergen, far to the north; to southern Argentina, far to the south; from the deserts of Utah in the west, to the Gobi Desert of China, far to the east.

Fossils of dinosaurs have been found in lands which are now covered with snow and ice much of the year; in lands where the hot desert sun blisters the earth and very little rain ever falls; in places as far apart as Africa and Australia.

Of course, conditions were very different upon the earth at that time. Deserts now cover areas which in many places were once lush, green, and swampy, with many streams and lakes. There was plenty of vegetation for the plant-eating dinosaurs to feed on, and thus plenty of these dinosaurs for the meat-eating dinosaurs to feed on!

11

Where did dinosaurs come from?

There is a difference of opinion among scientists on this question.

EVOLUTION

Some scientists, who are evolutionists, believe that dinosaurs evolved (slowly came into being by many in-between forms) from some kind of ancient reptile about 200 million years ago, and that they became extinct (died out) about 70 million years ago.

12

CREATION

There are other scientists, called creationists, who believe that the scientific evidence shows that dinosaurs did not evolve, but that they were created by God, just as described in the Bible. Creationists believe that dinosaurs were created the same time that Man and all other creatures were created, probably sometime less than 10,000 years ago.

The Bible says:

And God said, Let the earth bring forth the living creature after his kind, cattle, and creeping thing, and beast of the earth after his kind: and it was so.

And God made the beast of the earth after his kind, and cattle after their kind, and everything that creepeth upon the earth after his kind: and God saw that it was good.
Genesis 1:24, 25.

A description of the creation of Man, both male and female, follows in verses 26 and 27, and then verse 31 tells us that God saw everything that he had made, and it was very good — "And the evening and the morning were the sixth day."

Thus the Bible tells us that God made Man and the dinosaurs (included among the beasts of the earth) on the sixth day of creation. We should also mention that in the 21st verse of the first chapter of Genesis, it is mentioned that God created 'great whales' on the fifth day of creation. This same word is translated 'dragon' in other places in the Old Testament, so perhaps the marine reptiles were created on that day. Some might wish to call these creatures marine dinosaurs.

13

Is there scientific evidence that Man and dinosaurs lived at the same time? We have not yet found fossils of dinosaurs and fossils of Man together. Of course it is very unlikely that we will ever do so. First of all, it is very hard to find dinosaur fossils, even though many have been found. Most important of all, very, very few fossils of ancient people have ever been found. The probability of finding a fossil of a dinosaur and a fossil of a human being in the very same place is thus very, very, very, very small— so small in fact, that it will probably never happen, even though it is not impossible.

There are some people, however, who believe they have seen footprints of dinosaurs and Man together. In the rocky bottom of the Paluxy River near Glen Rose, Texas, footprints of dinosaurs have been found. Evidently dinosaurs had walked through a muddy area, leaving their footprints. The mud hardened quickly, and soon afterwards the footprints were covered with soil, brought in apparently by a flood. Before long, everything became very hard, turning into rock.

Thousands of years later, the Paluxy River began to run through this area and washed away the soil and rock on top of the footprints to uncover the footprints. This was possible because the rocky material which covered the footprints was softer and more easily eroded (washed away) than the hard rock in which the footprints were made.

Many years ago there were people who lived near Glen Rose, Texas, who said they had seen human footprints very close to the dinosaur tracks. A lot of people have gone down to Glen Rose to look for these human footprints. Some people claim they have found human footprints there but others claim that they have not been able to find any evidence for human footprints in that area. They believe that what the other people are claiming to be human footprints aren't really human footprints at all.

Are there human footprints and dinosaur footprints together in the Paluxy River bottom? We don't know. We will not be able to say absolutely sure one way or the other until more work is done.

The Bible gives us some other clues that Man and the dinosaurs lived at the same time, for in the Book of Job we find a pretty good description of a dinosaur, indicating that people in those ancient days, after the great Flood of Noah, still remembered dinosaurs. In Job, chapter 40, verses 15-24, we read:

Behold now behemoth, which I made with thee; he eateth grass as an ox. Lo, now, his strength is in his loins, and his force is in the muscles of his belly. He moveth his tail like a cedar: the sinews of his thighs are knit together. His bones are as strong pieces of brass: his bones are like bars of iron. He is the chief of the ways of God: he who made him can make his sword to approach unto him. Surely the mountains bring him forth food, where all the beasts of the field play. He lieth under the shady trees, in the covert of the reed, and fens. The shady trees cover him with their shadow; the willows of the brook compass him about. Behold, he drinketh up a river, and hasteth not: he trusteth that he can draw up Jordan into his mouth. He taketh it with his eyes: his nose pierceth through snares.

New Analytical Bible

16

This is a description of a mighty creature! Some have claimed that this is a description of an elephant, others have said it was a hippopotamus, but verse 17 tells us that this creature "moveth his tail like a cedar," or great tree. Have you ever seen the tail of an elephant?

This could not be a description of a hippo or of an elephant! But it does sound mighty like a dinosaur!

17

WHAT DID DINOSAURS LOOK LIKE?

All dinosaurs started out as eggs, since dinosaurs, like other reptiles, such as lizards, turtles, and crocodiles, laid eggs.

Many fossil dinosaur eggs have been found, especially in certain areas of China.

The mother dinosaur laid her eggs in some warm spot in soil or sand where the sun would help to keep them warm. In a few weeks, probably, the eggs would hatch, and the baby dinosaurs most likely had to take care of themselves right from the start.

There were all kinds of dinosaurs in those ancient days.
Little ones — no bigger than chickens!
Big ones — up to 90 tons (one hundred and eighty thousand pounds!)
  Plant eaters —
    Meat eaters —
      Some were armored —
        Some had spikes on their heads!
      Some had spikes on their tails!
  Some had long necks.
Some had short necks.

Now let's see what dinosaurs looked like!

19

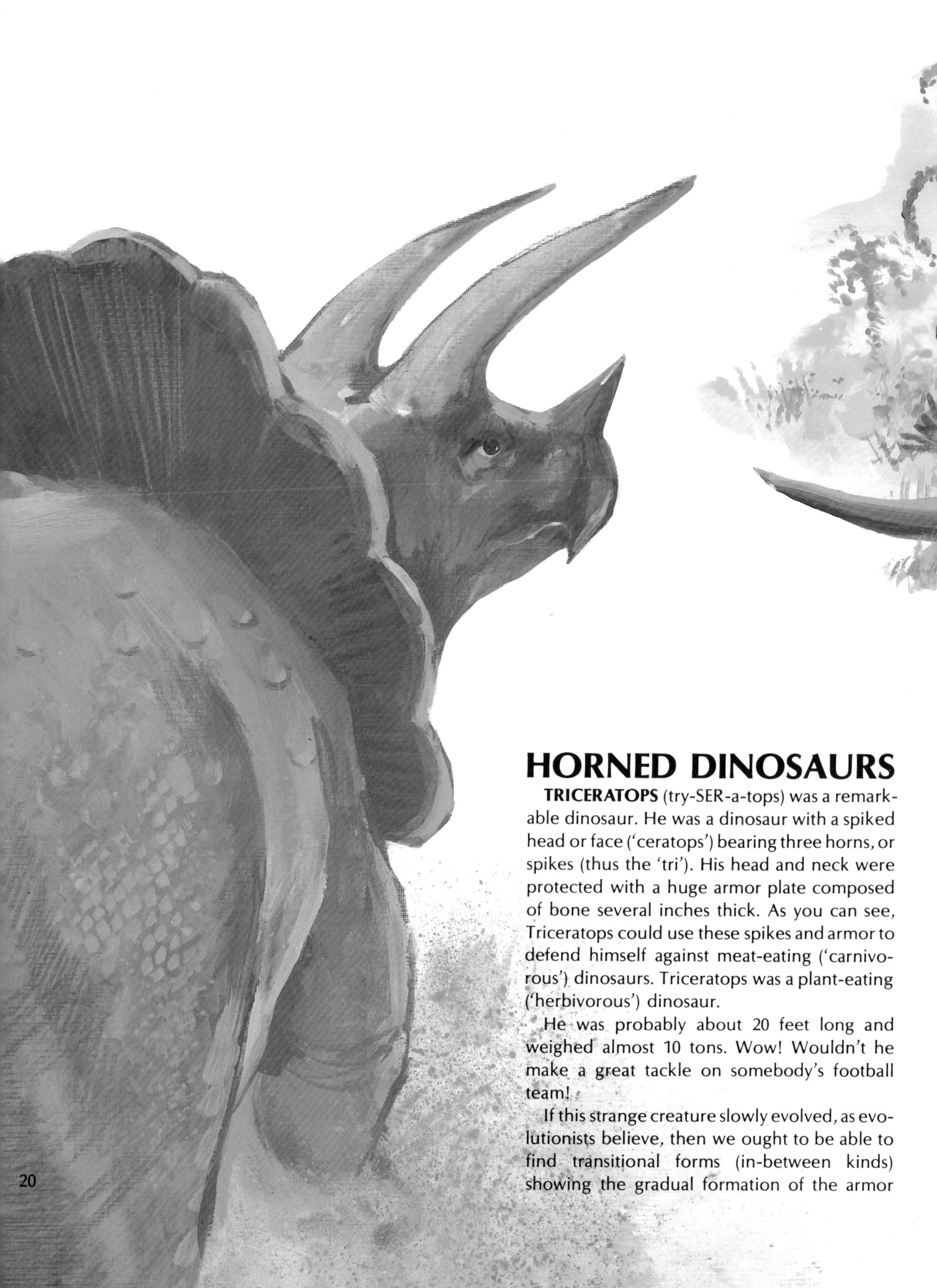

HORNED DINOSAURS

TRICERATOPS (try-SER-a-tops) was a remarkable dinosaur. He was a dinosaur with a spiked head or face ('ceratops') bearing three horns, or spikes (thus the 'tri'). His head and neck were protected with a huge armor plate composed of bone several inches thick. As you can see, Triceratops could use these spikes and armor to defend himself against meat-eating ('carnivorous') dinosaurs. Triceratops was a plant-eating ('herbivorous') dinosaur.

He was probably about 20 feet long and weighed almost 10 tons. Wow! Wouldn't he make a great tackle on somebody's football team!

If this strange creature slowly evolved, as evolutionists believe, then we ought to be able to find transitional forms (in-between kinds) showing the gradual formation of the armor

plate and the spikes, but none are found!

All of a sudden, here is the Triceratops dinosaur, complete, armor plate, spikes and all, just as we would expect if God had created this dinosaur. Nowhere do we find in-between forms with spikes starting out as little spikes which gradually got bigger and bigger, and finally ending up as a Triceratops dinosaur. The first time you see a dinosaur with armor plate on his head and with three spikes, he is a full-fledged Triceratops, with a huge armor plate and three big spikes. This is strong evidence for creation!

Those spikes are not made to hang things on, of course! They were terrible weapons with which this plant-eating dinosaur protected himself against meat-eating dinosaurs.

We can imagine what may have happened on some ancient battlefield. As several Triceratops are leisurely snipping off the tops of plants along the edge of a marsh bordered by a forest of palm trees and other kinds of trees, suddenly a hungry Tyrannosaurus rex, a giant meat-eater, comes crashing out of the forest toward the Triceratops. Most scramble for safety, but there is one that is so slow that he has no choice but to fight or be killed and devoured.

He faces the charging Tyrannosaur and waits until he is within range, and then, before the Tyrannosaur can rip open his side, he suddenly rears up and drives his spikes into the soft underbelly of the Tyrannosaur. The Tyrannosaur screams with rage and pain, and retreats to a safe spot to nurse his wounds and to wait for a less formidable creature to devour.

21

There was a variety of other horned dinosaurs. These included, for example, **STYRACO-SAURUS** (sty-rak-uh-SAWR-us). He had a long horn on his nose and six sharply pointed spikes sticking out from a shield of bone that projected back from his skull, protecting his neck and shoulder region. He, too, was provided with some highly effective armor plate and weapons. He wasn't exactly a buzz-saw, but he was just as dangerous!

PLATED DINOSAURS

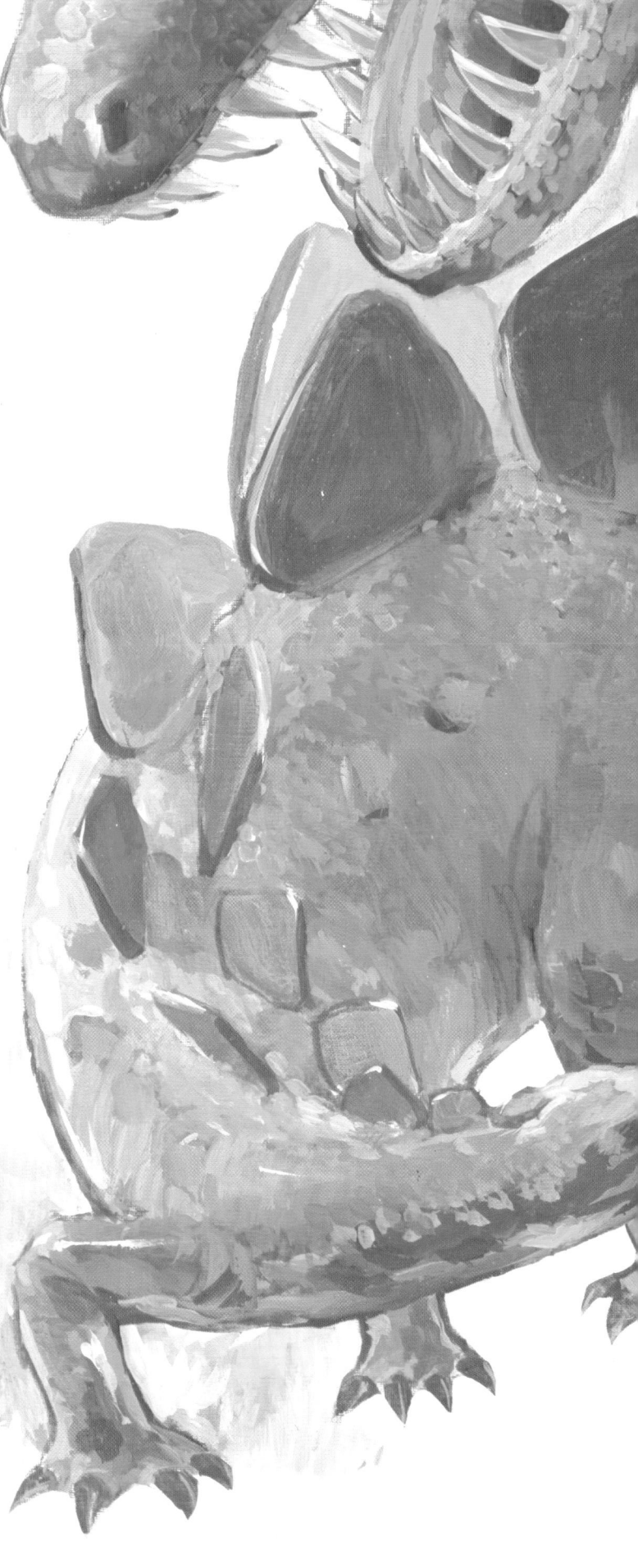

This is **STEGOSAURUS** (steg-o-SAWR-us). How different he was from Triceratops! He didn't have any spikes on his head, but look! He had four spikes near the end of his tail! These spikes were three feet long and six inches thick at the base.

They were even more terrible weapons than those of Triceratops because they could be whipped around by his powerful tail. I am sure you would stay clear of the tail-end of Stegosaurus!

Stegosaurus, a plant-eating dinosaur, was about 20 feet long and weighed almost two tons. But look at his head! It was tiny compared to that of triceratops, and the brain of the two-ton Stegosaurus was no bigger than a walnut. Probably in those days instead of saying 'dumb like an ox,' we would have said 'dumb like a Stegosaurus.'

But Stegosaurus, like some other dinosaurs, had extra 'brain power' in his rear quarters. Near his hips the spinal cord had an enlargement or knob that was 20 times as large as his brain. This really wasn't a second brain, as it is often called, but was a sort of computerized control center for his tail, hind legs, and rear quarters.

It provided this portion of his body with quick reflex actions without waiting for the nerve signals to travel 20 feet to the brain and 20 feet back to the tail. The brain in his head did all the real thinking, of course, and had control of the voluntary movements of the rear legs and tail.

As you probably have noticed, even though this dinosaur walked on all four legs [therefore called a 'quadruped' (quawd-ru-ped)], his rear legs were twice as long as his front legs. As a result his rear end stood eight feet high.

There was, of course, another very unusual feature about this dinosaur. He had a double row of bony plates (thus the name Stegosaurus — 'plate lizard.') that ran all along his back from his neck almost to the end of his tail. Some were as high as two feet and almost two inches thick. They were not fastened to the spine, but were anchored into the tough thick skin.

It seems obvious that these plates served as armor to help protect Stegosaurus against attack, but not all scientists agree about this. Some believe that these plates were heat exchangers, absorbing heat from the sun on a cool but sunny day, and giving off heat on a really hot day when Stegosaurus would find a shady spot to rest. (At any rate, they had a purpose!)

There were many times, no doubt, when a Stegosaurus had to defend himself against attack by one of the meat-eating dinosaurs. In this picture you see Stegosaurus whipping his spikes into an Allosaurus. Perhaps the Allosaurus finally won the battle and had the Stegosaurus for dinner, but he sure knew he had been in a fight!

These strange creatures, just like Triceratops, appear 'out of nowhere.' There are no transitional, or in-between, forms showing little spikes on the tail, gradually getting longer and longer in other in-between forms. There is no evidence for evolution here.

There are no series of in-between forms showing the bony plates along the back gradually evolving or coming into being. Not a single such in-between form can be found! Whenever a fossil Stegosaurus is found he is always a complete Stegosaurus, spikes, plates and all. This is good evidence that these creatures did not evolve but that they were created by God.

ANKYLOSAURUS (ang-kuh-lo-SAWR-us) had about as much armor as a General Sherman tank! In fact, his name means 'stiff lizard.' Not only were the head, neck, back, and tail of Ankylosaurus covered with large, round knobs of bone, but he had a war club for a tail! The tail of Ankylosaurus was thick and powerful and had a large round bony ball near the end.

When this fifteen-foot long dinosaur was approached by a dangerous enemy, he could crouch low and draw his feet in under his armor-plated back. And then when attacked, WHAMMO! He would slug the leg or head of his attacker, who had probably already broken a few teeth trying to bite through the armor of Ankylosaurus. Unless the attacker was able to somehow upend Ankylosaurus and roll him over on his back, he would have to go somewhere else to find his dinner, no doubt nursing some bumps and bruises!

There were other kinds of armored dinosaurs. Their fossils have been found in North and South America, Europe, and Asia. These include **POLACANTHUS** (po-luh-KAN-thus). He was a little smaller than Ankylosaurus. As you can see, he had a double row of large sharp horns running from his head back to his

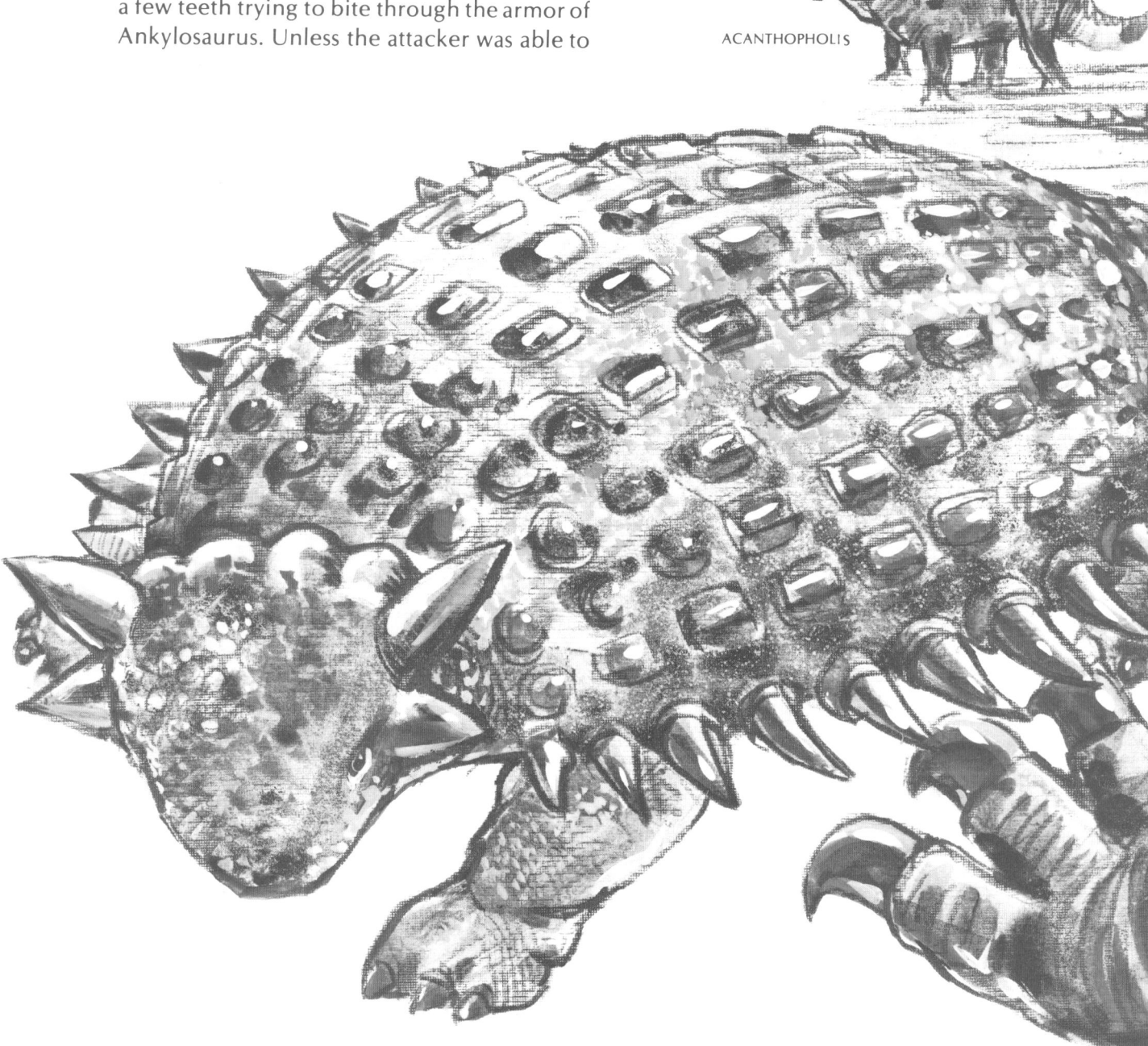

ACANTHOPHOLIS

26

hips, as well as a double row of flat plates which ran out along his tail. No doubt this was sufficient to give some of the meat-eating dinosaurs second thoughts about attacking Polacanthus.

These armored dinosaurs, with their various types of armor and spikes of different sizes and shapes, all appear in the fossil record completely formed the very first time their fossils are found. No in-between forms! That's because God created them.

PALEOSCINCUS

POLACANTHUS

DUCK-BILLED DINOSAURS

It is easy enough to imagine a bird with a duck-bill, but can you imagine a dinosaur with a duck-bill? But, there were dinosaurs with duck-bills! In fact, there were lots of duck-billed dinosaurs on the earth at one time, and there were several different kinds.

The most numerous of these duck-billed dinosaurs was the **TRACHODON** (TRAK-o-don). He was about 30 feet long and stood about 18 feet tall, big enough to look a Tyrannosaurus in the eye — but I'm sure he wouldn't want to do that!

The front part of Trachodon's jaws was flattened out like a duck's bill and was probably made up of horn-like material. Just as with a duck's bill, there were no teeth in this part of the jaw. He did have teeth, however. In fact, he had about 2000 teeth! These were all in the back of his jaw, 500 on each side of his lower and upper jaws. Many of the teeth were on top of others, so that as some wore out or fell out, they were immediately replaced.

The name Trachodon means 'rough-tooth' (another name given to Trachodon by some scientists is **Anatosaurus** (uh-NAT-uh-SAWR-us) which means 'goose lizard').

Trachodon must have been a good swimmer. He had three webbed toes on his hind feet and three webbed toes on his short front feet (he also had a fourth toe on each front foot). In addition to these webbed feet, he had a powerful flattened tail that no doubt helped to make him a good swimmer. The three webbed toes on both the front and hind feet ended in hoofs, so while he spend much of his time walking only on hind legs, he must have spent part of his time on all fours, at least when feeding.

Trachodon probably used his swimming ability both to feed and to escape his enemies. At times when there was only a scarce supply of plants along the shore, or perhaps when Trachodon simply desired a change in diet, he could swim out into lakes and streams and snip off plants growing along the bottom.

Trachodon always had to be alert for his deadly enemies — the meat-eating dinosaurs. When Trachodon was threatened by one of these creatures, he hastily splashed into the water and swam to safety in the middle of the lake or stream. That was probably his only defense. He certainly couldn't do any fighting with his duck-bill!

Two remarkable fossils of Trachodon found in Wyoming showed what the skin of these dinosaurs looked like. These creatures had been buried so quickly that their flesh did not have time to decay before they were completely buried in the mud. This mud formed a mold around these dinosaurs, and left an impression of exactly what they were like, including the skin.

These impressions show that these dinosaurs had no armor or hard scales of any kind for protection. It appears that they had a skin much like the modern day lizard known as a Gila monster. Probably these creatures were often killed and eaten by the large meat-eating dinosaurs.

There were several other kinds of duck-billed dinosaurs, and their duck-bills were not the only thing that made them look strange! They had some odd-shaped structures on their heads, indeed. Three of these are shown in the picture. As you can see, **CORYTHOSAURUS** (kuh-rith-uh-SAWR-us), which means 'helmeted-lizard,' had a semi-circular bony crest on top of his head that looked like a helmet. Except for this feature he probably looked a lot like Trachodon. One fossil of this creature showed that he was about 18 feet long.

LAMBEOSAURUS (lam-be-uh-SAWR-us) had a crest on top of his head shaped like a hatchet. I guess we should call him ole hatchet-head! He was named after a geologist by the name of Lambe.

PARASAUROLOPHUS (par-uh-sawr-AHL-uh-fus), which means 'like-a-crested-lizard,' had a long curved bony tube that stuck way out behind his head. No one really knows what purpose was served by this bony crest or those on Lambeosaurus and Corythosaurus. Scientists have offered several different ideas. The bony structures on all of these dinosaurs were hollow and were connected to their noses by tubes. Some have suggested that they were chambers for storing air, allowing these dinosaurs to stay under water for longer periods of time. Others have suggested that these bony humps or crests gave the duckbills a better sense of smell. Some have even suggested that these crests were noise-makers which allowed them to bellow or to trumpet out loud noises. That would have made it possible for them to warn their fellow duckbills when a meat-eating dinosaur appeared. Most scientists admit that they really don't know what purpose was served by these strange hollow structures. We don't either, but later on when we talk about 'dragons,' we are going to make an interesting suggestion!

There were other kinds of duck-billed dinosaurs. All appear in the fossil record fully-formed, with no transitional forms, or in-between kinds, just as would be expected if God created them. If they had evolved slowly and gradually over many millions of years, as evolutionists believe, we should be able to find many in-between kinds, but none are found!

BONEHEAD and PARROT-LIZARD

Because of their small brains, dinosaurs probably were not very smart. We might be inclined to think of them as 'boneheads'. Well, there was one dinosaur that was a *real* bonehead. His name is very long and hard to pronounce — **PACHYCEPHALOSAURUS** (PAK-ee-SEF-uh-luh-SAWR-us). The name means 'thick-headed lizard.

He was given this name because he had a bony dome on top of his head about 10 inches thick. He had only a tiny brain, so the name 'bonehead' would fit him in more ways than one. He must have been dumb, even for a dinosaur!

Pachycephalosaurus not only had a bony dome, but he had odd-looking bumps and spikes of bones on his head and face. He probably was quite an ugly critter. He was about 20 feet long and ate plants.

PSITTICOSAURUS (sit-uh-ko-SAWR-us) was only about four feet long, not very big compared to most dinosaurs. His name means 'parrot lizard.' He got his name from the fact that he had a parrot-like beak.

31

MEAT-EATING DINOSAURS

And now we want to talk about the meanest, fiercest, most terrible dinosaurs of all — the carnivorous, or meat-eating, dinosaurs. There were many different kinds and sizes of these meat-eating dinosaurs, but we will only talk about the two most interesting ones, Allosaurus and Tyrannosaurus.

ALLOSAURUS (al-lo-SAWR-us) was the smaller of these two dinosaurs, but he sure wasn't any midget! In fact, he was about 35 feet long and stood nearly 15 feet high. He had terrible jaws and teeth, for his head was 2½ feet long, and he had many teeth, all 3 inches long. His jaws were especially built so he could open them very wide in order to gulp down large chunks of meat.

As you can see from the picture, he had large and powerful hindlegs, each of which had three toes with long sharp claws. His small forelimbs also had three toes, or 'fingers,' each of which had claws. He appears to have been well-equipped, indeed, to kill and eat other creatures.

32

He probably dined on reptiles and dinosaurs of all kinds and sizes, some of which he killed with one snap of his powerful jaws and then downed in a single gulp or two.

If he chose to have an armored dinosaur, like Stegosaurus, or a huge dinosaur, like Brontosaurus, for dinner, the story might be quite different, of course, and the outcome might be somewhat in doubt.

Let's imagine, for example, that he has found a Brontosaurus (we'll learn more about this monster later), and has decided to kill him to satisfy his raging appetite.

Perhaps this Brontosaurus has been feeding on plants growing along the shore of a lake. Meanwhile, our Allosaurus, ravenously hungry, has been lurking in the woods near the lake, listening and looking for a victim. He hears Brontosaurus crashing through the shallow water along the shore.

Using one of the large paths leading to and from the lake, Allosaurus hunts for his intended victim as quietly as his huge size permits. Finally, when he is as near to Brontosaurus as possible without being seen, he suddenly lunges forward with the greatest speed possible.

Brontosaurus, caught by surprise, does not have time to seek the safety of deeper water. He has time only to make a few desperate defensive moves. He is not made for fighting, for he has no claws, and his teeth are not long and sharp like those of Allosaurus, but are short and flat for eating plants.

He is very big, however, and has a very large and powerful tail. As Allosaurus charges, he swings his huge tail at Allosaurus as quickly and powerfully as he can, hoping to knock Allosaurus off his feet. This would give him time to flee to deeper water, or perhaps would give him an opportunity to crush or cripple Allosaurus by crashing his huge body down on his enemy.

But Brontosaurus is too slow. Before his thrashing tail can knock Allosaurus flat, Allosaurus has leaped upon his back, with his claws sinking deep into the flesh of Brontosaurus. The teeth of Allosaurus flash terribly as he opens his huge jaws, and with one powerful snap he sinks his teeth deep into the neck of Brontosaurus, almost completely cutting through his spinal cord.

Thrashing wildly, Brontosaurus falls as Allosaurus again and again slashes at his throat. Finally, Brontosaurus lies still and lifeless.

Allosaurus begins his feast, tearing away huge chunks of flesh and gulping greedily. When he has gorged himself full, he slowly leaves the scene, seeking some cool spot to rest and sleep until hunger once again calls him to the hunt.

The most terrible killer of all the dinosaurs was **TYRANNOSAURUS** rex (tye-ran-o-SAWR-us). His name means 'king tyrant lizard.' He indeed was the king of the tyrant lizards. In some ways, he was twice as large as Allosaurus. His huge head was 5 feet long, and his teeth were 6 inches long and sharp as daggers. It has been estimated that he could open his mouth four feet wide!

His powerful body was about 50 feet long (longer than a railroad boxcar), and he stood about 20 feet tall. He probably weighed about 10 tons, or 20,000 pounds. Wouldn't he be something in a circus!

He had very large and powerful hind legs, with three toes on each foot. Each of these toes had a claw 8 inches long. His front feet were very small, too short, in fact, to reach his mouth. Each had only two toes, or 'fingers.' Scientists are not sure just what help these forelimbs were to Tyrannosaurus.

Many fossils of the duck-billed dinosaurs have been found near the fossils of Tyrannosaurus, so it is probably a safe guess that a duck-billed dinosaur often provided a meal for Tyrannosaurus. From time to time he also probably dined on a huge plant-eating dinosaur similar to Brontosaurus.

Many of the armored dinosaurs, such as Ankylosaurus, and the horned dinosaurs, such as Triceratops, were also available, but as we have already described, these horned and armored dinosaurs could put up a mighty powerful fight, powerful enough, perhaps, to convince Tyrannosaurus to seek his dinner elsewhere.

There were other meat-eating dinosaurs, some middle-sized and some small. At least it is assumed they were meat-eaters, because of the kind of teeth and jaws they had, although some scientists believe that all dinosaurs were plant-eaters. All that is left of these dinosaurs are their fossils, of course, so sometimes we just have to guess about some of these things.

When did these animals become meat-eaters, if indeed they were meat-eaters as most scientists believe? Genesis 1:29-30 indicates that as originally created, man and all animals were to be plant-eaters only. We believe it is very likely that some animals, such as the dinosaurs, lions, tigers, etc., became meat-eaters after sin came into the world. We know that many other changes took place at that time. For example, the Bible tells us (Genesis 3:18) that thorns and thistles came into being at that time. Whether these animals were able to change naturally into meat-eaters merely by a change in the kind of food they liked, or whether God had to change them, we do not know.

Some day be sure to visit one of the great natural history museums that are found in such cities as Los Angeles, Chicago, Denver, and New York City. Then you can stand in front of the fossils of one of these huge creatures and try to imagine just what he was like and what he must have eaten for food! You might even shiver a little bit as you look up at the huge gaping jaws of Tyrannosaurus rex and imagine him chasing after you for an in-between-meal snack!

BIG PLANT-EATERS

It is time now to talk about the huge plant-eaters. We will start with **DIPLODOCUS** (dih-PLAHD-o-kus). As you can see, he was a long dinosaur, in fact, possibly the longest one that ever existed. He was almost 100 feet long, or as long as a string of 10 elephants standing head-to-tail. That makes some tall tale! He weighed about 25 tons, considerably less than either Brontosaurus or Brachiosaurus, but still a monster.

You will notice that much of his length was made up of the very long neck and very long tail. In fact, his name means 'double beam,' and comes from the fact that his neck and tail each resemble a beam of nearly equal length, sort of like the two beams, or arms, on a balance that is used to weigh things.

Although some toes had claws, he had broad pads on his feet like an elephant. His front legs were about the same length as his hind legs. He walked on all fours, so he was a 'quadruped.'

Supposing Diplodocus got bit on the end of his tail. Imagine how long it would take for the message to reach his brain, and for the return message to get back to his rear quarters, telling his tail muscles to jerk his tail away! So what do you think God the Creator did about that? Well, of course, just as was the case with Stegosaurus, there were 'secondary' brains' or knobs (called 'ganglia') along the spinal cord of Diplodocus.

Thus, if Diplodocus got bit on the end of his tail, the painful message had to travel only as far as the knob on his spinal cord near his rear legs in order for a message to bounce back to his tail muscles, saying 'jerk!'

In fact, we might say Diplodocus was sort of a 'jerk' anyhow, because he had such a tiny brain. He was quite harmless, though (as long as he didn't step on you!), and spent his days peacefully munching on plants that lived along the shore or in the water.

That is, his days were peaceful unless one of the meat-eating dinosaurs showed up! In that case, Diplodocus would hastily move into deep water, using his long neck to keep his head above water while he sheltered himself in the depths of the lake or river.

38

And here is the most famous dinosaur of all. Everybody knows who he is. **BRONTOSAURUS** (BRAHN-to-SAWR-us)! Of course! Just about everyone assumes that Brontosaurus was the biggest dinosaur that ever lived. I suppose that's because he is the biggest that most of us have ever seen in a museum. Well, he was big, alright — 70 feet long or so, standing about 20 feet high at the shoulders, and weighing about 40 tons, or 80,000 pounds! But as we will see shortly, he was out-weighed two-to-one by another dinosaur!

Brontosaurus means 'thunder lizard.' He was probably given that name because the person naming him thought the ground would rumble like thunder while Brontosaurus was rambling around. It is believed that he had to eat several hundred pounds of food every day to satisfy his huge appetite. That's a lot of plants! In fact, he probably didn't do much else but eat and sleep.

This picture will give you a better idea just how big a Brontosaurus was. Look at that foot-print! Big enough for a bathtub!

A lot of dinosaur footprints have been found, from those of the huge Brontosaurus to those of dinosaurs no bigger than chickens. As described earlier when we were talking about the footprints found near Glen Rose, Texas, fossil footprints can form when footprints are made in mud which quickly hardens into rock, and then is covered over by a mixture of mud, sand, and gravel which is brought in by a flood.

Many thousands of years later, erosion (washing away) by rivers removes the stuff that covered the footprints for us to see. After many years, of course, the footprints will slowly disappear as they gradually, in turn, are eroded away. It would take a long time for this big Brontosaurus footprint to disappear!

Here is the biggest dinosaur of all time — **BRACHIOSAURUS** (BRAK-ee-o-SAWR-us). At least he's the biggest anyone has found yet. It is believed that he weighed up to 90 tons (180,000 pounds), more than twice as much as Brontosaurus.

He was about 80 feet long, and you can see one reason he was that long — his very long neck! He stood about 20 feet high at the shoulders, but his head was held almost 40 feet in the air, as high as a four-story building. Fossils of this dinosaur have been found in North America, Europe, Africa, and possibly in Asia, so he really got around.

He was a mighty monster of a dinosaur, alright, but his brain was no larger than that of a little kitten! You sure didn't need much brains to get by in those days! That is, if you were a dinosaur. But just like Diplodocus, Brontosaurus, and many other dinosaurs, Brachiosaurus had extra 'brains,' or nerve cord knots, along his spinal cord to act as fast-reaction communication centers for his parts that were a long way from his real brain. Unlike most dinosaurs, the front legs of Brachiosaurus were longer than his hind legs (his name means 'arm lizard').

Another peculiar feature about Brachiosaurus was the fact that his nostrils were not out on the end of his nose, or snout, like most other animals, but were located in a bony dome on top of his head. When he got chased into deep water by one of those big meat-eating dinosaurs, all he had to do to get a breath of air was to raise his head high enough to get that knob out of the water — just like the periscope of a submarine!

Now I wonder how evolution could have been clever enough to think up that idea, and then to gradually move the nostrils from the nose, where it was located in his supposed ancestors, up into the dome on top of his head?!!

In fact, no fossil in-between forms can be found for these dinosaurs showing their gradual evolution from some little fellows. They ought to be found, however, if evolution is true. These dinosaurs appear in the fossil record complete as Diplodocus, Brontosaurus, and Brachiosaurus when we first find them, because God created them just like that. Again and again the facts fit creation and show that evolution theory is false.

IGUANODON

IGUANODON (ih-GWAHN-uh-don) was also a plant-eating dinosaur. He had some peculiar features, but what made him one of the most famous dinosaurs of all was the fact that he was the first dinosaur ever found. That happened more than 150 years ago.

Until that time, no one knew, of course, that dinosaurs had ever existed. A few fossil bones of dinosaurs had been found, and a few fossil footprints had been seen, but people thought that the bones had belonged to some big elephant or other large animal, and that a giant bird had made the footprints.

Dr. Gideon Mantell was an English doctor who liked to collect fossils. One day in the spring of 1822 his wife was taking a walk in the country when she saw what appeared to be a big tooth among the rocks. She knew about fossils, of course, and she knew this might be important, so she brought it to her husband. He had never seen anything like this before. He looked around for more, and not only found more teeth but also a few bones.

Since he had no idea what kind of an animal this was, he sent the teeth and bones to Baron Cuvier, a famous French scientist and an expert on fossils. But this time Baron Cuvier's educated guess was wrong. He thought that the teeth were from an ancient rhinoceros and that the bones were from an extinct hippopotamus.

Not long after this, Dr. Mantell showed the fossil teeth to someone who was familiar with the iguana, a lizard that lives in Mexico and South America. Although the fossil teeth were much, much larger, his friend declared that they looked just like the teeth of the iguana. Dr. Mantell decided that he had found the remains of an amazing new kind of animal, a giant plant-eating reptile-like animal. He gave it the name Iguanodon ('iguana-tooth').

Soon afterward the fossil bones and teeth of a huge meat-eating lizard-like animal were discovered. The creature was given the name Megalosaurus. It was now realized by most scientists that this creature and Dr. Mantell's Iguanodon belonged to a newly-discovered kind of ancient creatures that no longer roamed the earth. Someone with imagination thought up the name 'dinosaur' and thus dinosaurs were here to stay!

Scientists still did not know exactly what Iguanodon had looked like, because they had found only parts of his skeleton. A sharp beak-like bone had been found, and it was supposed that this had been fastened to the nose of the Iguanodon.

In 1877 an amazing discovery was made that told everybody what Iguanodon was really like. In a coal mine in Belgium, miners found the fossilized skeletons of 23 Iguanodons all piled up together. All kinds of suggestions have been made as to how this huge pile of dinosaurs met a sudden end, along with all those plants that somehow got changed to coal.

We believe that most likely they were suddenly destroyed and buried by the great world-wide catastrophe known as Noah's flood and described in the Book of Genesis.

Animals and plants don't become fossils unless they are buried quickly. If their remains just lie out on the ground or in water, everything gradually disappears, flesh, bones, teeth and everything. Many huge piles of bones have been found at spots all around the world, giving evidence for a great world-wide flood.

From the fossils found in the coal mine it was possible to reconstruct what Iguanodon really looked like. He was a big dinosaur weighing six to eight tons or so, about 30 feet long and standing about 15 feet high. He walked upright on his two hind feet, so he was a 'biped.' He didn't have a horn or beak on his nose, as was earlier supposed. The 'beak' turned out to be a thumb!

How do you suppose he used those sharp dagger-like thumbs? Your guess would be as good as anybody's, because nobody really knows. Maybe he used them to scratch his back! Most likely he used them to defend himself against other dinosaurs that liked to have Iguanodon steak for dinner, although they wouldn't have been much help against such giant meat-eaters as Tyrannosaurus.

THE LIGHTWEIGHTS

There were several dinosaurs that were similar in several ways to the ostrich. They were all lightweights, or perhaps we should call them bantamweights. Some were as large as an ostrich, but some were no larger than a rooster. They were all bipedal, walking on two legs. Their hind legs were long and slender, but their front legs were short. These three-toed front feet served as 'hands.' They all had toothless beaks like an ostrich.

STRUTHIOMIMUS (STROO-thee-o-MY-mus), which means 'ostrich-mimic' or 'ostrich-imitator' was probably more like an ostrich than the others. He was about eight feet tall, the same as an ostrich. He had a small head that sat on the top of a long slender neck. He had long, slender, but powerful legs. Unlike an ostrich, he had slender arms instead of wings, a leathery skin instead of feathers, and he had a long reptilian tail.

Although he had no teeth, Struthiomimus no doubt used his beak for snapping up worms, insects, and lizards which he would have to gulp down without chewing. Perhaps he ate plants also, just as ostriches do. We can imagine Struthiomimus rooting around for worms and insects with his front feet as well as with his powerful hind feet, and gobbling up lizards that were unfortunate enough to be within reach. He may even have dug up the eggs of other dinosaurs and feasted on the contents.

Struthiomimus didn't have much in the way of defense as far as weapons are concerned, but he did have a very powerful defense — speed. He could probably run faster than a racehorse. Of course, his problem was not racehorses, but the meat-eating dinosaurs. None of them, certainly none of the big ones, could run nearly as fast as Struthiomimus, so all Struthiomimus had to do to escape these meat-eaters was to keep a sharp lookout and move away at the first sign of danger.

ORNITHOMIMUS (or-NITH-uh-MY-mus), which means 'bird-mimic,' was very similar to Struthiomimus. In fact, some people believe they were probably one and the same. Fossils of both have been found in North America.

PODOKESAURUS (PO-duh-kuh-SAWR-us), which means 'swift-footed lizard,' was only about two to three feet long. Little **COMPSOG-NATHUS**, (kahmp-SAHG-nuh-thus), was no bigger than a rooster. These dinosaurs probably grubbed around just like chickens do today, and perhaps added small lizards to their diet too.

OVIRAPTOR (o-vuh-RAPT-or), which means 'egg-stealer,' was given that name because some scientists (certainly the one who named him!) believe eggs may have made up an important part of his diet. He was about three feet long, and fossils of this dinosaur have been found in the Gobi Desert of China where many fossil dinosaur eggs have also been found.

In fact, it has been reported that the bashed-in skull of an Oviraptor was found among fossilized dinosaur eggs. Maybe Oviraptor was caught in the act of eating an egg, and was done in by the snap of the jaws of the angry dinosaur who had laid the eggs!

LIZARD HIPS

ALLOSAURUS

BRONTOSAURUS

TRACHODON

STEGOSAURUS

BIRD HIPS

48

ANKYLOSAURUS

ANCESTORS FOR BIRDS?

We have said many times in this book that fossil hunters have not been able to find the transitional forms, or in-between kinds, that we ought to find if evolution were true. Instead, each one of these many different kinds of dinosaurs appear in the fossil record already complete as if they came out of nowhere, just as we would expect if they had been created.

But wait! Don't these lightweight dinosaurs we have just been talking about look mighty like an ostrich, especially Struthiomimus? Wouldn't he make a good in-between form between dinosaurs and birds, especially if some feathers were added?

Unfortunately for evolution theory, there is something very wrong with these dinosaurs if we try to make ostriches out of them. There are two basic kinds of dinosaurs. These are the 'lizard-hipped' dinosaurs (Saurischia) and the 'bird-hipped' dinosaurs (Ornithischia). We won't try to explain the differences here, but it is obvious that the lizard-hipped dinosaurs had hip bones that were shaped like those of lizards, and the bird-hipped dinosaurs had hip bones similar to those of birds.

The ostrich is a bird, of course, and most evolutionists believe that ostriches evolved from earlier birds that could fly. Ostriches have bird hips, just as we would expect. But what about the 'ostrich-like' dinosaurs we have been talking about? Everyone of them was a lizard-hipped dinosaur! None of them, therefore, could have been the ancestor of the ostrich. They had the wrong kind of hips.

The bird type hip suddenly appears in certain kinds of dinosaurs, with no in-between forms showing where the bird-hip came from. That's because God created them!

Is it possible that one of the bird-hipped dinosaurs could have been the ancestor of birds? Well, what kind of dinosaurs were bird-hipped dinosaurs?

Ankylosaurus was bird-hipped — but he surely couldn't have been the ancestor!

Stegosaurus was bird-hipped — the ancestor of birds? No way!

Trachodon was bird-hipped — 30 feet long, 18 feet high, with huge feet with hoofs and a big alligator-like tail. No ancestor here!

Parasaurolophus, Corythosaurus, and Lambeosaurus were bird-hipped dinosaurs. Look at their pictures. They were very large, up to 30 feet long, with large heavy hind legs, big heavy tails, and large bony structures on their heads. They were pretty good swimmers but were not the kind of creatures that could have produced the birds!

Iguanodon was also a bird-hipped dinosaur. No possible ancestor here!

In fact, all of the dinosaurs that had long slim legs, small lightweight bodies, and in general appearance looked somewhat like birds, were all lizard-hipped. On the other hand, the dinosaurs that were bird-hipped were otherwise all wrong to be the ancestors for birds. These facts are difficult to understand if we assume evolution is true, but they surely don't present any problems for scientists who believe in creation!

TRICERATOPS

PARASAUROLOPHUS

CORYTHOSAURUS

LAMBEOSAURUS

DRAGONS and BOMBARDIER BEETLES

What? Dragons? Everybody knows that dragons never existed! and what in the world could a beetle possibly have to do with a dragon anyhow?

Well, we don't know whether or not dragons really existed, but we believe there is a chance that they did, and the little half-inch long bombardier beetle helps us to understand how dragons may have 'snorted fire!'

Legends are stories about things that happened long, long ago — things that happened long before the people telling the stories were even born. Nobody can really know, then, whether or not the stories are true, because nobody now living was there to see whether those things actually happened. Many legends, however, are believed to be about things that really did happen, although every little thing in the story may not be true.

It is probable that legends that are told by people in many different parts of the world are about things that really happened. It would be hard to believe that the same story could have been made up by different people all around the world.

For example, not only is the story of a great flood that covered the entire earth found in the Bible, but similar stories are told by many different kinds of people all around the world, people who could not possibly have heard about it from the Bible. A story of a great flood that destroyed almost everybody was told by ancient Chinese, and long, long ago by South American Indians, North American Indians, ancient Greeks, and other peoples scattered around the world. These stories, therefore, must be about something that really happened.

Stories about dragons also were very common long, long ago, all around the world. The stories, therefore, must have been about animals that really lived. Even the Bible tells about animals that could have been dragons.

There is a terrible animal, called a 'leviathan,' that is described in Job, chapter 41. It must have been an animal that lived both in the water and on the land. The Bible tells about the uselessness of trying to catch him with fishhooks (v. 1) or with harpoons (v. 7), and tells us that he made the deep water boil like a pot with his commotion (v. 31). This means he must have spent at least part of his time in the water.

The Bible also tells us in verse 26, however, that neither swords nor spears could stop him. Swords could only be used against an animal on land. Perhaps, then, he could come out on land, also.

The most interesting thing about this great and powerful creature is described in verses 18 to 21. Listen to what the Bible says:

> When he sneezes, he gives out a flash of light. His eyes are like the rays of the dawn. Out of his mouth shoot flames, from him fly sparks of fire. Out of his nostrils comes smoke like a pot heated over brushwood. His breath sets coals on fire, and a flame pours from his mouth.

Job 41:18-21 (American Translation — Beck)

Wow! That sounds mighty like a dragon, doesn't it! What else could it have been?

But how could such a creature generate fire? What kind of chemistry did he use to do that? To find a possible answer, let us go back to the bombardier beetle.

The bombardier beetle, given the scientific name **BRACHINUS** (BRAK-uh-nus) by zoologists (scientists who study animals), is only about one-half inch long, but he has a mighty powerful weapon with which to fight off his enemies.

When an enemy comes up close behind him — **BOOM!** An explosion goes off right in the face of his enemy, and irritating and bad-smelling gases shoot out from two tail tubes at a very hot 212°F (as hot as boiling water!). Oh boy! That's enough to discourage any mean ole beetle-eater, isn't it?

How in the world does a little beetle manage to shoot fiery hot gases out of twin tail tubes, and just when he needs it to keep from getting gobbled up by a mean ole beetle-eater?

A German chemist by the name of Dr. Hermann Schildknecht decided he was going to study the bombardier beetle to find out what kind of chemistry this marvelous little beetle uses to fire off his two cannons (I wonder how many bombardier beetles he had to catch to do that?).

This scientist found, first of all, that the bom-

bardier beetle mixes up two kinds of chemicals —hydrogen peroxide and hydroquinone.

Now the marvelous thing about this is, if you or I went into a chemistry laboratory and mixed up those two chemicals we would soon have a mess! Those chemicals react with each other to produce a dark-colored, dirty-looking liquid—a real mess.

But not so with the bombardier beetle. He's a smart chemist. When he mixes up these two chemicals he makes sure that he adds another kind of chemical, called an inhibitor. The inhibitor somehow prevents the other two chemicals from reacting together, and the mixture of these two chemicals remain as clear as water. The bombardier beetle stores this liquid mixture in two storage chambers, ready to be used when needed.

When a mean ole beetle-eater (Mr. B.E.) tries to sneak up behind the bombardier beetle (Mr. B.B.), Mr. B.B. squirts the chemical liquid (containing the hydroquinone and hydrogen peroxide) into two combustion tubes (firing tubes) that he has in his tail, while aiming at Mr. B.E. Then just as Mr. B.E. opens his mouth and is ready to snap up Mr. B.B., **BOOM!** He is frizzled by the explosion, which pours hot, irritating, and bad-smelling gases right into his face. Ugh! Even if Mr. B.E. weren't hurt very badly, he surely wouldn't want to eat anything like that for dinner!

How does Mr. B.B. make the chemical solution explode just at the right time, in spite of the fact that the solution contains an inhibitor which ordinarily keeps the hydrogen peroxide from reacting with the hydroquinone? Dr. Schildknecht found out that when the bombardier beetle squirts the solution into the combustion tubes, there are two chemicals in the combustion tubes which neutralize (knock out) the inhibitor. These two chemicals are enzymes called catalase and peroxidase (enzymes are chemicals that make chemical reactions go millions of times faster). When hydroquinone and hydrogen peroxide are mixed together with these two enzymes in the combustion tube, they react violently together and **Boom!**—they explode.

Now, let's see if we can possibly imagine how all this marvelous chemistry and beetle-boomer machinery could have slowly and gradually come into existence by evolution. Please remember that evolution supposedly takes place by lots of acci-

dents. Could a series of accidents (all of which are really nothing more than mistakes) gradually change an ordinary beetle into a bombardier beetle? No way!

Well now, let us see if we can dream up an imaginary evolutionary story about how the bombardier beetle may have evolved. Perhaps millions of years ago there was this little beetle. Let's call him Beetle Bailey. One day his Mom and Dad gave him a chemistry set for his birthday, and a little while later he decided to mix up some hydrogen peroxide, hydroquinone, and the enzymes to see what would happen.

So he did. Yep, you're right. **BOOM!** He blew himself up and splattered himself all over the walls of his chemistry lab. Poor little Beetle Bailey!

For a long time after that (according to our evolution story), for many thousands of generations (a generation is how long one family lives), and perhaps hundreds of thousands of years, little beetles were mixing up those chemicals and blowing themselves up—boom, boom, boom. You see, Beetle Bailey couldn't tell his children that little beetles shouldn't be mixing up those kinds of chemicals. He didn't live long enough to grow up and have beetle babies!

But on the other hand, how could everything have happened just in the right order by accident? Supposing that just by chance Beetle Bailey got hydrogen peroxide and hydroquinone. What good would they be to him? What would he do with them? He doesn't have the enzymes yet, so he couldn't make them explode. If he just had hydrogen peroxide and hydroquinone he could put them in a storage chamber (if he had one), but the inhibitor hasn't accidentally evolved yet. His chemical mixture just sits, sours, and turns into a dirty mess as it eats up his innards! That's no good for anybody, especially Beetle Bailey.

So now we can begin to see some of the problems for evolution. First, Beetle Bailey needs a storage chamber to store the chemicals, but why would he need a storage chamber until he had the chemicals? Why would evolution "invent" a storage chamber when there was no need for one? On the other hand, how could evolution "invent" the chemicals before there was a storage chamber in which to put them? And why would evolution "invent" the two chemicals and the storage chamber when there was no inhibitor to keep them from

eating themselves up and turning into a mess? And why would evolution "invent" the two chemicals, a storage chamber, and the inhibitor when all of that was no good anyhow?! Beetle Bailey couldn't use any of this against a mean old beetle-eater because the enzymes had not accidentally evolved yet and so he couldn't make them explode.

But now, in spite of all this impossible nonsense, supposing somehow, once upon a time, some little Beetle Bailey just did happen to invent hydrogen peroxide, hydroquinone, the inhibitor, the storage chambers, and the two enzymes. Oh boy! Finally, you will say, Mr. Beetle Bailey has become Mr. Bombardier Beetle. But not so fast! Supposing that this little beetle has a storage chamber with the two enzymes and he squirts in a big charge of the two chemicals and the inhibitor. **WHAMMO!!!** The enzymes knock out the inhibitor and cause the two chemicals to explode. **BOOM!** Once again Beetle Bailey has blown himself up and splattered himself all over the landscape.

You see, the problem is this. The combustion tubes haven't evolved yet. If Beetle Bailey had the combustion tubes, he could mix up everything in the combustion tubes and then when the mixture explodes it would shoot out of the combustion tubes without blowing up Beetle Bailey. But of course evolution doesn't "know" this. Evolution is the dumbest thing in the world! According to evolution, everything just gets invented by a bunch of accidents. But how could a bunch of accidents invent combustion tubes?

Those combustion tubes are really very special. They have to be strong enough to stand the force of an explosion. They have to be made of very special materials so that they don't get eaten up by those nasty chemicals, or get burned when those chemicals get as hot as boiling water. They have to be equipped with valves to release the pressure just at the right time. Wow! All of that couldn't just happen by accident! It would take a lot of smart engineers (or one Master Engineer) to know how to put all of that together.

And of course everything had to happen in just the right order. What good would it do if evolution invented the combustion tubes before all those chemicals and enzymes got accidentally invented? What on earth would Beetle Bailey do with those

combustion tubes? He couldn't use them for anything. On the other hand, how could evolution invent all those chemicals before the combustion tubes accidentally evolved? They would just explode and blow up poor little beetles. Boom, boom, boom! You see, **everything** has to be there right from the start before you can have a bombardier beetle.

Now you can see that evolution is really impossible, but in spite of all of this, let us suppose that somehow Beetle Bailey does, by a series of accidents (big laugh), just happen to end up with all those chemicals, inhibitor, enzymes, storage chambers, **and** the combustion tubes. Now you would say, Beetle Bailey has finally become Bombardier Beetle. He's all ready for action.

But wait! Not so fast! His communication system hasn't been invented yet. He can't give all the necessary signals at just the right time.

With a real bombardier beetle, things are very different, of course. You see, he has the chemicals stored in the storage chambers along with the inhibitor, while the enzymes are in the combustion tubes ready to go to work. When a mean ole beetle-eater begins to try to sneak up on the bombardier beetle, Mr. B.B. sends out some signals through his communication system. As soon as he spots the mean ole beetle-eater, he sends out signals that cause his tail-end with the combustion tubes to swivel around in just the right direction so that they are aimed at the mean ole beetle-eater (Mr. B.B. is always right on target—he never misses). Then just when the mean ole beetle-eater is in the right position, Mr. B.B. sends out signals and the mixture of chemicals are squirted from the storage chambers into the combustion tubes and **POW!** The chemicals explode, another signal opens up the valves on the combustion tubes, and those nasty gases, as hot as steam, pour out of the combustion tubes right into the face and mouth of the mean ole beetle-eater. Boy, that's enough to repel any kind of a would-be beetle-eater! The nasty ole beetle-eater back-pedals as fast as possible, gagging all the time, with his tongue hanging out. He'd had it!

That's the way it happens when everything is there—chemicals, inhibitor, storage chambers, combustion tubes, enzymes, and a very, very complicated communication system. But remember now, in our imaginary evolution story,

not everything is there yet. The communication system has not been invented yet. Boy, that could really be embarrassing for Beetle Bailey! He wants to be a real sharp Bombardier Beetle, but he has no communication system, he has no control. Supposing his friend Joe Beetle comes up and pats him on the back and says, "Hi, friend." **POW!** Poor J.B. The explosion goes off right into the face of Joe Beetle. Oh boy! Beetle Bailey is going to lose a lot of friends that way! For thousands of generations and hundreds of thousands of years, friends of Mr. Beetle Bailey were getting it right in the face. And, Beetle Bailey wasn't able to hit the mean ole beetle-eaters just at the right time, either.

All of this stuff—chemicals, inhibitor, storage chambers, enzymes, combustion tubes, and special valves—would be of absolutely no use until the communication system was complete and operating perfectly. On the other hand, what good would all of that complicated communication system be before all of the rest had been invented? Everything would have to happen in just the right order. In fact, **everything** had to be there before **anything** would be of any use at all.

Could evolution make all of that happen by a zillion accidents? Why the very idea is ridiculous! No way! Mr. Beetle Bailey couldn't have become Mr. Bombardier Beetle slowly and gradually by evolution. Mr. Bombardier Beetle had to be Mr. Bombardier Beetle from the very first moment, with everything perfect and complete.

That means he could not have evolved! He had to be created by a Creator who knew exactly what had to be there, and who created everything all at once. The bombardier beetle tells us that only God, the Master Engineer, could have created the bombardier beetle and all the other marvelous creatures that live on this earth.

But what does all this have to do with dragons?

Well, if a little half-inch long beetle can do all of that, why couldn't a monstrous 30-foot long dinosaur have a similar kind of chemical apparatus, or perhaps something even more fearsome?

Remember Corythosaurus, Lambeosaurus, and Parasaurolophus? These are the dinosaurs we described earlier (p. 30) that spent a lot of time both in the water and on land. They also had strange hollow bony structures on the top of their heads, connected by tubes to their nostrils. No one has ever been able to figure out what these hollow bony structures were used for.

Do you suppose one of these, or perhaps something similar to it, could have been the leviathan described in Job, chapter 41? Maybe this creature could mix some chemicals together similar to those used by the bombardier beetle, and store them in a storage chamber. Then when a meat-eating dinosaur like Tyrannosaurus came after him, he could squirt a big charge into his combustion chamber (the hollow structure on the top of his head?), add an anti-inhibitor at just the right time, and ZZZZZZZZZZZZZZ! Fire and smoke would come pouring out right in the face of the Tyrannosaurus. Boy, would his face turn red! He would surely go look somewhere else for his dinner!

It seems possible to us, then, that dragons really did exist long, long ago. They existed so long ago that ancient peoples could only remember them by the stories that had come down to them from their ancestors. Most likely no knight on a horse ever killed a dragon, though. That's the made-up part of the story!

WHATEVER BECAME OF THE DINOSAURS?

This is the question scientists have thought a lot about but have never really been able to answer. All kinds of ideas have been suggested, but none of them seem to fit all the facts. Nobody really knows why all the dinosaurs became extinct (died out). We don't know either, but we may have a good idea.

Some scientists have suggested that the dinosaurs, with their tiny brains, couldn't compete with the much more intelligent mammals. To many scientists, however, that idea does not seem likely at all. How could the 40-ton Brontosaurus, or the large ferocious Tyrannosaurus, be killed off in the battle for life by mammals weighing only a few ounces or a few pounds?

Others have suggested that egg-eating mammals ate so many dinosaur eggs that dinosaurs died off much faster than they were being born, and so they finally died out completely. That doesn't explain, however, why some reptiles, such as turtles, snakes, lizards, and crocodiles, did manage to survive, or why flying reptiles and reptiles that lived in the sea (marine reptiles) also died out at the same time the dinosaurs died out, in spite of the fact that they probably could lay their eggs where the mammals couldn't get them. It is even possible that the baby sea reptiles were born alive in the water rather than hatching from eggs laid on a sandy beach.

Various other ideas have been suggested to explain the death of all the dinosaurs, such as disease, glandular trouble, cosmic rays from the explosion of a star (a supernova), and changes in the magnetic field of the earth. Most recently some scientists have suggested the idea that perhaps an asteroid struck the earth. Supposedly this monumental collision threw billions of tons of dust into the air, blacking out the sun for several years and causing most plants to die, and so the dinosaurs died out for lack of food. Other scientists argue strongly against this idea. In fact, none of these ideas seems to be scientifically reasonable.

The idea suggested most often by scientists to explain the extinction of dinosaurs is the suggestion that the weather all over the earth changed so drastically that the dinosaurs simply could no longer survive in this "new" world. Perhaps the lush, plenteous vegetation that covered the earth at that time disappeared. This caused the plant-eating dinosaurs to die out. The meat-eating dinosaurs then died out because they had no plant-eating dinosaurs to eat.

We believe this to be a very reasonable explanation. There is a lot of evidence to prove that the world at one time did have a world-wide mild, or warm, climate. Greenland, which is now covered all year long with snow and ice, at one time had a sub-tropical climate much like that of Puerto Rico and other islands in the Caribbean. We know that because of the kind of fossil animals and plants that are found on Greenland. Fossils of plants and animals that now live only in warm or mild climates are found up in the far north above the Arctic Circle, and far south down in the Antarctic. This means that these lands, which are now frozen all the time, were once as warm as Kansas.

Just think! A world with no frozen Arctic or Antarctic. A world when Greenland was a near-tropic land with palm trees, and Canada was almost as warm as Florida. No icebergs. Lush vegetation covering much of the world. What a

place for the big plant-eating Brachiosaurus and all the other dinosaurs! In fact, there would be plenty of food for all the animals, including man.

But what happened? What happened to change the climate all over the world so drastically? What could have happened to change Greenland from a beautiful, warm, green, tropical paradise into a frozen wasteland, and the lovely green Arctic and Antarctic areas into lands of perpetual ice? What happened to the climate of the world that changed the playlands of the dinosaurs in China and Utah into deserts? What caused the Ice Age?

A lot of ideas have been suggested, but when all is said and done, scientists have to admit that they really don't know. We can't really say we know either, because we weren't there when all this happened. We believe we have a pretty good idea, however, what happened to the earth to make the weather change so drastically. We believe the Bible gives us the answer.

In the Book of Genesis the Bible tells us about a great flood that covered the entire earth and wiped out all people and land animals, except those on the Ark. It was this flood, or what caused the flood, that changed the climate of the earth. How did it do that?

Water vapor is water in the form of an invisible gas; like that, for instance, which collects on the outside of an ice-cold glass of water. We have rain when water vapor in the sky (atmosphere) condenses (forms moisture or droplets of water) and falls down to the ground.

If all the water vapor now in the atmosphere of the earth condensed and fell in the form of

rain over the entire surface of the earth, only about one inch of rain would fall and then there would be no water vapor left. The atmosphere would be bone-dry. This would be true, of course, only if the rain covered the *entire* earth.

The Bible tells us, however, that it rained very hard over the entire earth for at least forty days and forty nights during the great flood of Noah. This would bring down many, many inches of rain. The Bible also talks about the breaking up of the great deep. This means the crust of the earth broke up. Probably, as a result, the land sank down and the ocean floors came up (perhaps even large continents broke up to make smaller ones!). All of this along with the rain caused all of the land to be flooded by water. Even the highest mountains were covered.

If there is only enough water vapor in the atmosphere today for one inch of rain to fall (this would last only about one hour), but it rained hard for forty days and forty nights during the flood, there had to be a lot more water vapor in the atmosphere before the flood than after the flood. Because of this, the weather would have been much warmer before the flood than after the flood. Why do we say this?

Water vapor absorbs and helps to hold in the heat from the sun. When the atmosphere has a lot of water vapor in it, it is warmer than when it has very little. Therefore, the atmosphere before the flood, which had a lot of water vapor, would have absorbed and held more heat from the sun than does our atmosphere today, which has much less water vapor. This would have made the earth warmer than it is today, because the warm atmosphere would have acted like a warm blanket.

Because of this big change in atmospheric conditions at the time of the flood, the world became drier and cooler. The North and South Poles became lands of perpetual ice, and Greenland changed from a tropical paradise to a frozen wasteland. Lands that had been lush and green turned into deserts. The oceans became cooler.

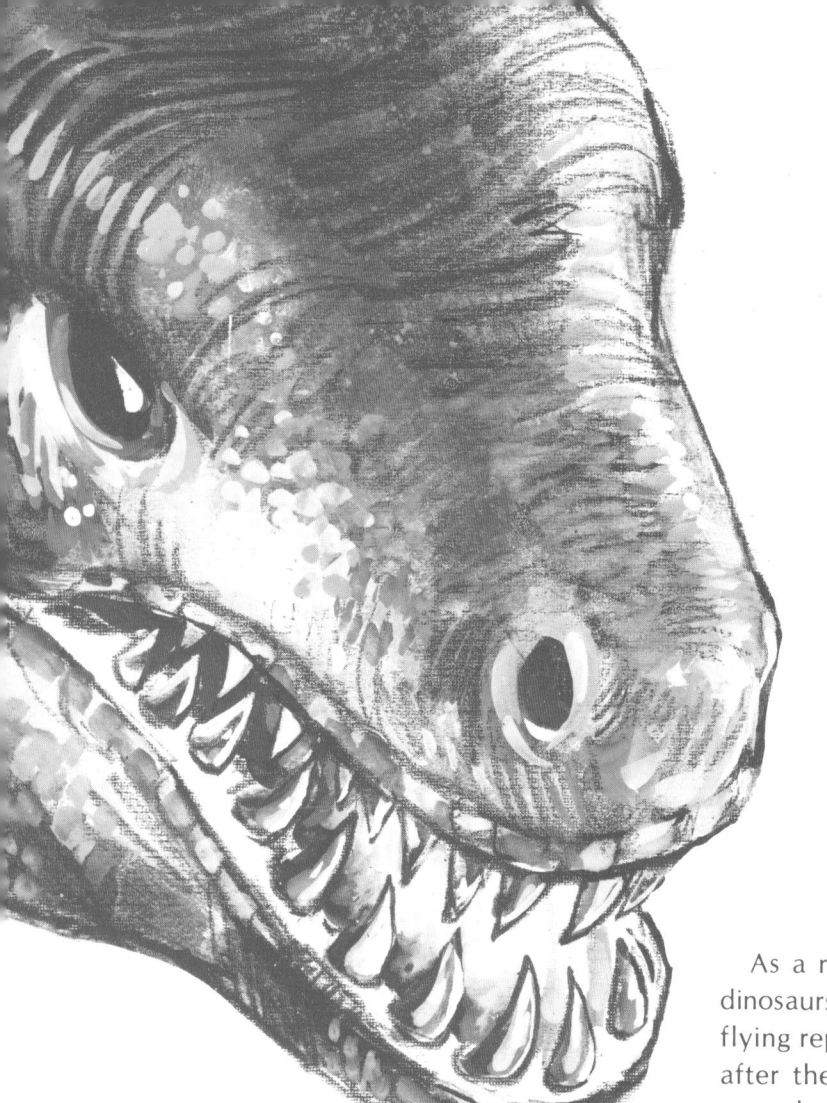

As a result of this change in the earth, the dinosaurs (and many other creatures, such as the flying reptiles and the sea reptiles) all died out after the Flood. They failed to multiply and spread around the earth. Since none have been found as yet, it is believed that none are still alive today. All we have left to tell us about dinosaurs are their fossil bones, fossil footprints, and fossil eggs.

But what an exciting story these dinosaur fossils tell us! Don't you agree that it is a lot of fun reading and thinking about dinosaurs?

Are you sad that they are all gone?

Maybe we should be glad.

Tyrannosaurus!

Brrrrrrrr!

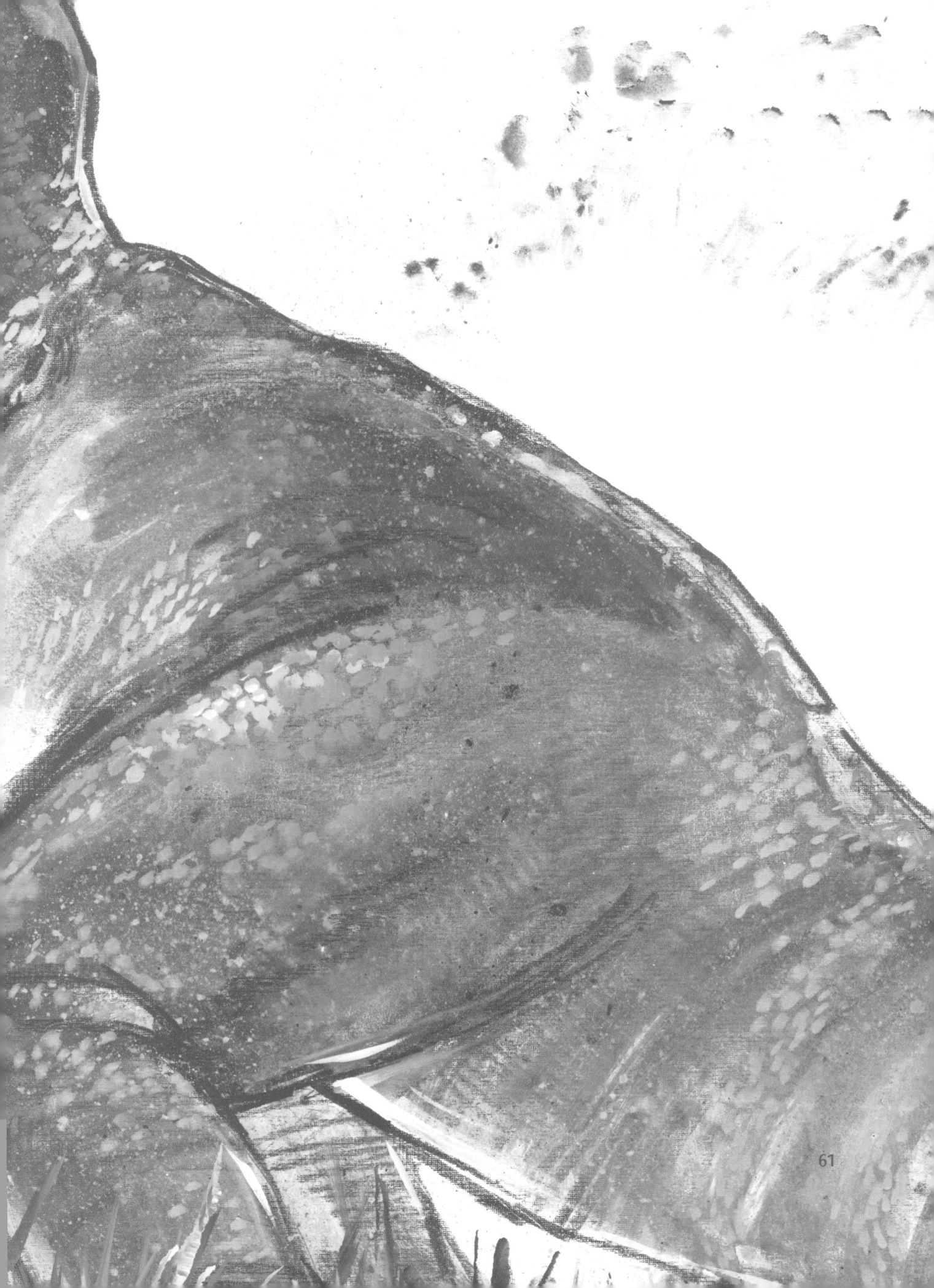

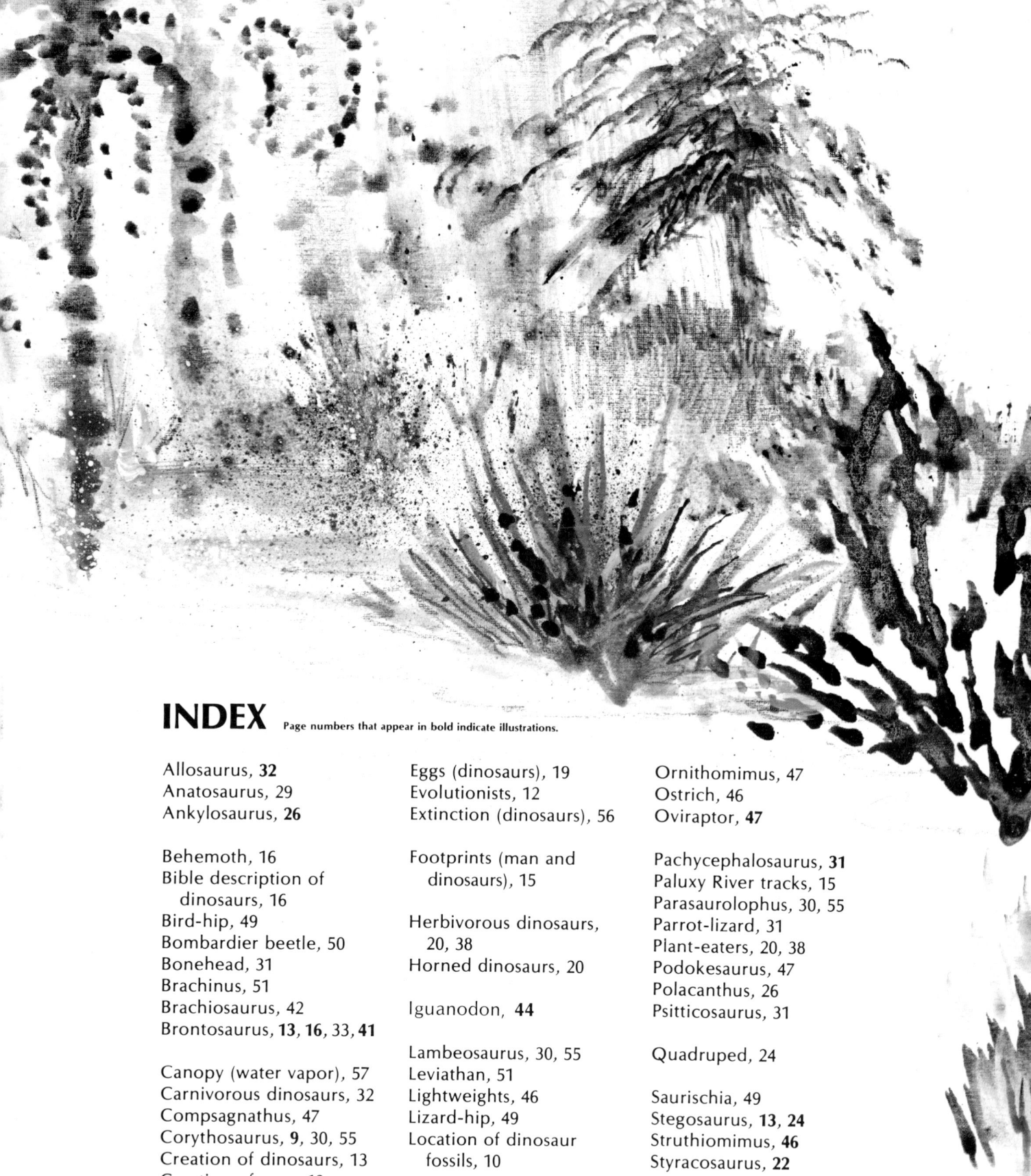

INDEX

Page numbers that appear in bold indicate illustrations.

Allosaurus, **32**
Anatosaurus, 29
Ankylosaurus, **26**

Behemoth, 16
Bible description of
    dinosaurs, 16
Bird-hip, 49
Bombardier beetle, 50
Bonehead, 31
Brachinus, 51
Brachiosaurus, 42
Brontosaurus, **13**, **16**, 33, **41**

Canopy (water vapor), 57
Carnivorous dinosaurs, 32
Compsagnathus, 47
Corythosaurus, **9**, 30, 55
Creation of dinosaurs, 13
Creation of man, 13
Creationists, 13

Diplodocus, **38**
Dragons, 50, 55
Duck-billed dinosaurs, 28

Eggs (dinosaurs), 19
Evolutionists, 12
Extinction (dinosaurs), 56

Footprints (man and
    dinosaurs), 15

Herbivorous dinosaurs,
    20, 38
Horned dinosaurs, 20

Iguanodon, **44**

Lambeosaurus, 30, 55
Leviathan, 51
Lightweights, 46
Lizard-hip, 49
Location of dinosaur
    fossils, 10

Meat-eating dinosaurs, 32

Noah's flood, 57

Ornithischia, 49

Ornithomimus, 47
Ostrich, 46
Oviraptor, **47**

Pachycephalosaurus, **31**
Paluxy River tracks, 15
Parasaurolophus, 30, 55
Parrot-lizard, 31
Plant-eaters, 20, 38
Podokesaurus, 47
Polacanthus, 26
Psitticosaurus, 31

Quadruped, 24

Saurischia, 49
Stegosaurus, **13**, **24**
Struthiomimus, **46**
Styracosaurus, **22**

Thunder lizard, 41
Trachodon, **13**, **28**
Triceratops, **13**, 20
Tyrannosaurus rex, **8**, 21,
    37, **61**